The Worry Antidote

The Practical Mystic's Guide to Living Fearlessly

Henry Thomas Hamblin

Hamblin Vision Publishing

© Copyright 2024 by Hamblin Vision Publishing - all rights reserved.

The content contained within this book may not be reproduced, duplicated or transmitted without direct written permission from the author or the publisher.

Under no circumstances will any blame or legal responsibility be held against the publisher, or author, for any damages, reparation, or monetary loss due to the information contained within this book, either directly or indirectly.

Legal Notice:

This book is copyright protected. It is only for personal use. You cannot amend, distribute, sell, use, quote or paraphrase any part, or the content within this book, without the consent of the author or publisher.

Disclaimer Notice:

Please note the information contained within this document is for educational and entertainment purposes only. All effort has been executed to present accurate, up to date, reliable, complete information. No warranties of any kind are declared or implied. Readers acknowledge that the author is not engaged in the rendering of legal, financial, medical or professional advice. The content within this book has been derived from various sources. Please consult a licensed professional before attempting any techniques outlined in this book.

By reading this document, the reader agrees that under no circumstances is the author responsible for any losses, direct or indirect, that are incurred as a result of the use of the information contained within this document, including, but not limited to, errors, omissions, or inaccuracies.

Contents

Concise Biography of Henry Thomas Hamblin By John Delafield, Hamblin's grandson	V
Introduction by Noel Raine	XVIII
Foreword by Henry Thomas Hamblin	XX

Part 1: The Antidote for Worry

    1. The Antidote for Worry   2
    2. Don't Worry About Worry   6
    3. Thought Control   10
    4. The Antidote   15

Part 2: Release From Fear

    5. Overcoming Fear   30
    6. The Inward Power   33
    7. The Power of the Infinite   36
    8. Self-Mastery   39
    9. Doing the Things We Fear   42
    10. Making Friends With Life   45

11. Putting It into Practice	48
12. In Tune with the Universe	56
13. Our Eternal Nature	61

Part 3: Making Friends With a Friendly Universe

14. Making Friends With a Friendly Universe	66
15. The Open Door	69
16. Seeing God	72
17. Knowing and Illusion	76
18. One Law, One Principle	81
Also by Henry Thomas Hamblin	83

Concise Biography of Henry Thomas Hamblin

By John Delafield, Hamblin's grandson

Who was Henry Thomas Hamblin?

Henry Thomas Hamblin was a spiritual teacher and writer based in Sussex, England, whose message and vision were straightforward and pragmatic. He believed that the spiritual life and the practical, everyday life were inseparable. His teachings centred around the power of thought and the importance of meditation to draw on the inner power, wisdom and love that we all have deep within us. Hamblin referred to this as "the Secret Place of the Most High" in the days before meditation was widely practiced in the West.

Hamblin was colloquially known as HTH, and later 'The Saint of Sussex'. Whilst his teachings leaned towards esoteric Christianity, his philosophy was truly universal, embracing the truths of all faiths. The emphasis of his message is on finding the power of spirituality within us all, in the context of our everyday lives, rather than religion. As a young man, he reacted against the dogma of his strict, religious upbringing, and believed that religion often divided people, while spirituality united people. His teachings came from a place of pure empathy and compassion for humankind.

Henry Thomas Hamblin worked right up to the end of his life in 1958 and left a legacy that continues to this day, its voice as much needed now as it ever was.

A Wayward Child

Henry Thomas Hamblin was born in 1873 in Walworth, South East London, of Kentish parents, and was the second of two sons. His father was very religious, and his grandfather a minister of the Baptist Church. His mother, although of diminutive size, was reportedly "great of soul" and ruled the family with benevolent autocracy. The family was poor, very poor, like all those living around them in that district of London in the late Victorian era, and, despite their hard work, the only education that could be afforded for Henry was an elementary one. He followed this with a course in technology, which proved to be of inestimable value to a youth who was considered by his parents and teachers to be wayward.

"Unstable as water; thou shall not excel," his mother reproached him regularly. No doubt she intended it to shame her son into a regime of self-improvement, in keeping with child-rearing practices of the time, but it was hardly confidence-inspiring! "Slacker!" was the repeated insult from his elder brother. Wiser, more objective, heads might have paused for long enough to recognise a certain potential in the young boy who, at the age of nine, could attempt the writing of a school newspaper. He had also established himself as something of an elocutionist. Writing and speaking would both prove valuable skills in later life.

His adolescent years gave little indication of an error in the family verdict. "Henry the wayward" moved from one poorly paid post to another, idled in between dead-end jobs, succumbed to bouts of ill-health, and, before he had reached the age of eighteen, had displayed more than the usual "adolescent failings", according to his autobiography, *The Story of My Life*. From a modern perspective, all these Victorian euphemisms point to Hamblin being something of a "bad lad", an impression added to by his own heavy hints that he had been no stranger to drinking and carousing. He suffered terribly from pangs of regret following his periods of over-indulgence, so that "Henry the sinner" became "Henry the saint" – until the next time. His pronounced rebellious streak landed him in hot water more than once. He constantly pushed against the boundaries of the fire-and-brimstone brand of Christianity in which he had been raised, which he felt to be unbearably restrictive. Reading about his struggles with authority as a young man somehow makes the rather aloof spiritual writer he became more accessible and endearing; it's hard not to warm to someone who so openly confesses their own faults and shortcomings, especially in the tightly buttoned-up era in which he lived. He was inspired by books, many of which fired his worldly ambition and prompted his spiritual imagination.

What his parents and educators overlooked was that Hamblin was a young man with huge aspiration, flushed with a youthful zest for life, and inspired by a worthy ambition to rise above the rut of his circumstances. Although he pushed against his father's dogmatic and punitive style of practising religion, at heart, he was deeply religious. A person's early environment, education, and adolescent behaviour can often determine the course of their life. Youthful indulgences of one sort or another are inevitable. Hamblin's studies of the New Testament, which revealed that selfishness and hypocrisy, rather than indulgence, received greater condemnation by Jesus, would have been very much in his consciousness.

A Successful Businessman

There is no doubt that Hamblin had an enquiring mind, and this, coupled with a desire for scientific accuracy, enabled him to achieve success in his later endeavours in business. In this, despite his lack of education, he was bolstered by boundless faith and courage, which, coupled with a shrewd business sense, ensured that he succeeded beyond all expectation. In 1898, having taught himself opthalmics at night, he qualified as an optician and set up his first successful business as an optician, Theodore Hamblin (now Dolland and Aitchison), frequented by royalty, the rich and the famous.

Hamblin was a natural entrepreneur and a born risk-taker. By this time, he was also a family man. He married Eva Elizabeth in 1902, and they went on to have two sons and a daughter.

He enjoyed acquiring several businesses, all with insufficient capital, and relying on credit and goodwill. He took more pleasure in the thrill of the challenge than in the promise of monetary gain. Far from being downcast in the face of numerous setbacks, he thrived on negotiating obstacles which appeared insurmountable. As soon as the business was established and running smoothly, however, rather than being satisfied with financial security and the ability to provide for his family, Hamblin's interest started to wane. He felt a loss of the initial drive and motivation, his physical and mental health began to decline… until the next big idea came along and away he would charge again, all fired up and raring to go.

Throughout all his wild days of youth and high-risk business ventures, Hamblin felt a great tug towards discovering a deeper meaning to life, beyond that of the daily struggle to make ends meet. Propelled by his discontent, he became a driven seeker after truth. In his quest, he met other prominent thinkers of the time and formed lasting friendships.

As his business success grew, so did a gnawing sense of depression. It was as if there was something inside him that had not yet found a voice. Around this time, he discovered the New Thought movement and began to read their publications. Hamblin realised then that none of his worldly success had made him happy. He felt that a move from London to the coast would be beneficial. Shortly afterwards came the outbreak of the First World War, and Hamblin went off to serve his country, leaving his business in the care of others, almost with a sense of gleeful relief, strange though it sounds.

But it was the sudden and unexpected death of his younger son at the age of ten, in 1918, that brought him to rock bottom and to question everything.

A Very Practical Mystic

Hamblin was not a genius, and millions of other people have made good in the world with even less promising assets. But it was in the second half of his life, when Hamblin turned away from creating highly successful business enterprises to focus instead on the spiritual realm, that his unique combination of the pragmatic and the profoundly spiritual shone forth. He has sometimes been described as a very practical mystic.

Hamblin began writing in the 1920s. The words seemed to flow from him. He found that writing clarified his thoughts. One of his first books written in this new phase of his career was *Within You Is The Power*, which was to sell over 200,000 copies. Other books soon followed. Hamblin believed that there is a source of abundance which, when contacted, could change a person's entire life. As long as people blamed their external circumstances for any misfortune, they were stuck in the 'victim role'; but if they moved in harmony with their inner source, their life could be full of abundance and harmony.

Soon after this, Hamblin set up a magazine called *The Science of Thought Review*, based on the principles of Applied Right Thinking. He wasn't discouraged by the fact that he had no experience of editing or publishing. His experience had taught him that if the mind worked in harmony with the Divine, then everything you needed flowed towards you. Anyone with any business sense at all knew that to set up a magazine with a first print run of 10,000 copies would be a risky thing to do. But Hamblin was not risk averse, to put it mildly! He wanted to put what he believed into practice. The only magazine of its kind in the 1920s, it soon gained a worldwide readership. Among his friends and contemporaries that were to contribute to the magazine were Joel Goldsmith, Henry Victor Morgan, Graham Ikin, Clare Cameron and Derek Neville, all of them prolific and successful writers. Apart from his international subscribers, Hamblin had close ties to comparative spiritual thinkers in many other countries, especially in the U.S.

Although he had been brought up in a strictly religious family, he hadn't found any of the answers he sought in the Church. He realised that, rather than following any creed or dogma, which didn't work for him anyway, he had to look within himself. He found contact with 'Presence' and realised it held the key to the peace he was seeking. All the time, his search was leading him nearer to discovering the way his thoughts affected his performance and outlook.

During the General Strike of 1926, the Great Depression of 1929-32, and again in years after the end of the Second World War, many homeless, unemployed wayfarers came to the Hamblin household seeking relief and shelter. Henry and Elizabeth provided them with a simple meal, new boots and clothing, and money for the road. Known colloquially as 'The Saint of Sussex", Hamblin was a man who applied his spiritual principles to his everyday life. Practical Mysticism was Hamblin's life's work. He helped people in deeply practical ways to become less fearful, happier, and more successful in their lives. To this end, he wrote books like *The Antidote to Worry*. However, later in life he realised that whilst these books genuinely helped people, they were largely concerned with the personality. He then wished to go a step further and become more fully a truly 'practical mystic', so he wrote a spiritual course of 26 lessons, each with a definite theme presented in a systematic way. This was designed to move beyond the constraints of personality so that the soul could breathe the pure air of Spirit. What was needed, he felt, was 'a total surrender of ourselves to the Divine.' The course is available as the book *The Way of the Practical Mystic.*

The Power of Thought

Hamblin was at the forefront of the New Thought movement which was gaining pace in the early 20th century. He discovered that 'new thought' was, in fact, ancient wisdom, based upon the truth that has always existed since before time began. All great souls give voice to that timeless truth in a myriad of different ways. Hamblin urges us to "Think in harmony with the Universal Mind." In other words, he underlines the fact that truth is and cannot be changed depending upon our mood or our whim.

Hamblin realised that we need not only a positive frame of mind but an applied way of thinking - Right Thinking, as he termed it. What did he mean by that? Well, he wrote a book on it, *The Little Book of Right Thinking*, which is in its 17th reprint. Essentially, he defines Right Thinking as:

- Thinking from the Divine standpoint.

- Controlling the thoughts so they do not go off on negative tangents away from the Divine Truth, which is always positive.

- Replacing negative thoughts with positive thoughts

- Living in the consciousness that all is well; and as an adjunct to this, remembering that perfection exists as a reality now, and to think in the consciousness of that knowledge.

- Meditation or prayer is the highest form of Right Thinking.

- Ultimately, however, the aim is to get beyond thought, 'to enter ultimate Truth'.

He says, 'When we cease thinking, we glide out on the ocean of God's Peace. Thought brings us to the foot of the mountain after which we have to proceed by intuition'.

> *'Health, Wealth and Happiness. Isn't this something we all want, either for ourselves or for those dear to us? And yet, how many of us are struggling*

to reach or hold such a goal for a sustained period of time?'

Hamblin's teachings explain how we can achieve all of these things, not by hard work and striving but by a simple change of thought. *Within You is the Power* is one of his simple but profound statements, and the title of one of his books.

Hamblin was a prolific author and had many thousands of followers studying and benefiting from his teachings and courses until his death in 1958. The simple principles contained in those teachings are as relevant today as they were when he was alive, and can still help us to achieve health, prosperity and happiness if we apply them conscientiously.

He died in 1958 in Chichester Hospital. The Hamblin Trust exists to this day to propagate the legacy of his work.

The Relevance of his Teachings Today

Hamblin was, essentially, a Christian mystic, yet his ideas about the simplicity and clarity of presence seem incredibly contemporary. He believed that the source of all wisdom is within us and all around us, and that this is the fundamental reality; there is no separation, and we are all one. His message and advice to all who read his work is that it is for everyone and is in harmony with the aspiration of all good people throughout time. Hamblin believed that there can be no finite creed of an infinite faith. Moreover, he suggests that, when creeds appear, true faith can be constrained.

He cautioned that if you seek God in prayer, the corollary is that you must have faith in Him. He often stressed that no prayer goes unanswered, and, although you may not get the answer requested, your prayer will be answered in some form. God is around us and within us, and this is the fundamental reality. He made it clear that, although human organisations come and go, God's laws are eternal, and that God is the quintessence of love, wisdom, and harmony. He expresses the clear view that "Blessed are they who believe and yet have not seen". The knowledge that God is born within us is fundamental to our understanding, and only by the loss of self can God be found. At the point a person surrenders his or her 'self' to God, it is then that a re-birth takes place and one's real life in God begins.

Some may question this view and ask: "What is this but the core teachings of the many brands of Christianity?" In response, Hamblin's view was that modern Christianity is a heterogeneous compound of the teachings of Jesus interwoven with historic pagan-based doubts and fears, litanies, supplications and more, all of which are closely guarded by a priestly hierarchy. These were strong views, and Hamblin does not disparage those who found them uncomfortable, as he says that churches are necessary and helpful for those who are succoured by them. Hamblin had a lifelong rebellious streak where authority was concerned, and this included the strictures of the Church. Hamblin would sometimes say that the Truth of the message of Jesus was so often wrapped up in dogma and creed that its purity and simplicity were obscured.

In his teaching, he states that first comes purity of intention, reminding his readers that one cannot serve God and Mammon. Either you trust God completely or you hedge your bets by having worldly alliances and a healthy bank balance. He maintains that trying to achieve both will impair spiritual development. Secondly, an individual's dedication to following God's path will require great patience, perseverance, faith and courage; but in following this path, the individual will develop forbearance and good will. He adds that other life experiences will follow naturally and lead to a developing compassion, which will enable the individual to radiate the love of God.

Where should we place Hamblin in the long line of mystics, seekers and finders? Perhaps it is rather impertinent to pose the question some 65 years after his death, but it is surely relevant to consider this point as, by any measure, he was an extraordinary person.

Remember that he was born into a life of poverty and obscurity but, despite a very limited education, by superhuman efforts of his imagination, he rose to wealth and secured an esteemed position in life, while all the time being aware of another "self" within him, a spiritual self. Dramatically, in the middle part of his life, he surrendered his material successes to follow his wider calling as a disciple of God. In this later life, he did not subscribe to any specific creed or form of religion. He was no haloed saint in the traditional sense, but he would have said, "What I have done, or rather what has been done through me, can be done by any person in the world according to their gifts and personal faith".

The essence of this teaching is that the latent power of God lies within everyone.

John Delafied is the grandson of Henry Thomas Hamblin and a retired RAF pilot. The majority of his childhood was spent living with his grandparents, Henry Thomas and Elizabeth Eva Hamblin.

Introduction

BY NOEL RAINE

HT Hamblin was a prolific author of a range of books, booklets and pamphlets offering practical advice on how to live in harmony with God, or what he sometimes referred to as *Source, the Universe,* or *the Cosmic*. However, this was not just a spiritual quest, or an attempt to avoid the troubles and cares of everyday life – far from it, for Hamblin was a very practical mystic – but a practical guide to each one to follow to increase health, happiness, and prosperity.

Hamblin founded the *Science of Thought Institute*, offering a course of practical lessons intended to guide his many thousands of students towards a happier, healthier and more prosperous life and, although he is sadly no longer with us in person, he left a wonderful legacy of publications that he had written from 1921 up to the time of his death in 1958. Some of those are still in print and available from **The Hamblin Trust** on www.thehamblinvision.org.uk but many have since gone out of print.

Conscious that the Trust will not be around forever, the custodians of Hamblin's teachings, the trustees of **t**he Hamblin

Trust, have decided to produce copies of Hamblin's earlier works in digital format to leave a legacy for future generations. Whilst the style of writing may now seem a little dated, Hamblin's teachings remain valid and, although edited a little to bring them more into line with current editorial style, we are pleased to bring to you in one compilation, three of Hamblin's original booklets concerning fear, worry and anxiety:

- Release from Fear (First published in 1934)

- The Antidote for Worry (First published in 1951)

- Making Friends with a Friendly Universe (First published in 1956)

It is our hope that this compilation will, indeed, help **you** to make friends with a Friendly Universe and experience a life free from fear, worry and anxiety.

Many blessings for health, success and happiness.

Noel Raine

Chair of the trustees

The Hamblin Trust

Foreword

by Henry Thomas Hamblin

The object of issuing this little book is to provide a practical manual on the subject of fear and how to overcome it. It is not a learned or scientific treatise, for the writer has no claim either to learning or scientific knowledge. Instead, it describes in plain language those methods which have proved efficacious in the case of the author. His only qualification is that, up to a few years ago, he was a victim of fear of the worst type, and through the simple methods described in this book, he has been set free. On the principle that an ounce of practice is worth more than a ton of theory, this little work is offered to the attention of those whose lives are being spoilt by fear, and who desire, more than anything else, to be delivered from its bondage and power.

H.T.H.

Part 1: The Antidote for Worry

Hamblin Vision Publishing

Chapter One

The Antidote for Worry

Because I am a child of God, all my needs are supplied according to His riches in glory by Christ Jesus.

Philippians 4:19

When discussing any subject, the first thing for us to do is to define our terms.

The strict meaning of the word **antidote** is: *a medicine given to counteract a poison*. Thus, a person who has taken poison, does not have the poison extracted from him, but he's given something which neutralises the action of the poison, so that it can have no harmful effect. We shall keep to this strict definition for reasons which will become apparent later.

The strict meaning of the word **worry** is: *to keep on biting, to mangle, to choke, to pull about with the teeth, as with dogs fighting, molesting sheep, etc.* The worry with which we shall deal will be the same idea applied to thought. Worry, for the purpose of this article, will therefore be the action of uncontrolled thoughts which keep on biting, pulling about, and destroying our peace of mind, like a sheep being worried and pulled to pieces by wild dogs.

Let us bear these two definitions in mind while considering this matter, as they are necessary to a proper understanding of the subject. We are all agreed that worry does no good; but, probably, few of us realise how great and how far reaching are the evil effects of this destructive habit.

First of all, allowing thoughts of apprehension, care, fear, etc. to enter the mind destroys our peace of mind. Because our peace of mind is destroyed, we cannot think normally. Not only can we not think calmly and sanely, but we may even become irritable, which is a sure sign of instability. This, in turn, destroys the happiness of the home, and the harmony which should always exist in our work. These are two disasters; for the first is the most precious possession of man, for it is so valuable no money can ever purchase it; and the second is almost as important, for upon the harmony that man creates in his sphere of work depends his livelihood.

Our Mental Atmosphere

A person who is given to worry carries with him an atmosphere which depresses and irritates other people. Even if he keeps his worries to himself, instead of inflicting them on others, the mental atmosphere is present, affecting others and estranging them. Thus, a person may think that another person's irritability is entirely the other's fault, whereas it may be his own discordant mental atmosphere that may be the cause.

It is not difficult to see that if a man lives in a mental atmosphere which repels other people, he can never be much of a success in his home, and that he is unlikely to be successful in his business or profession. So much depends upon an attractive personality. The one with a healthy mental atmosphere attracts people and opportunities, whereas the reverse becomes the case if his mental atmosphere is gloomy, fearful, and depressed.

If a man gives way to the worry habit the quality of his work suffers. His true success in life depends ultimately on the quality of his work. But if he worries, then he cannot turn out that quality of work which life demands of him, and which is due from him. Consequently, there comes a time when he has to suffer for this. He may think that he is badly used and unfairly treated, but he is only being rewarded according to his work. As he looks back, if he is candid and sincere, he sees that it is all the result of his having given way to worry. If he had overcome his worry habit, he would have turned out better work, and better work would have brought correspondingly good reward.

The Effect of Worry on the Nervous System

But, the evil effect of indulging in worry, or allowing destructive thoughts to dominate him, does not stop at this point, for it not only destroys his peace of mind, it also lowers the standard of his health. The effect of worry is to wear down and exhaust the Nervous System. When the Nervous System becomes exhausted any disease to which we may be subject may develop. The health of every organ depends upon the quality of the blood, and a healthy Nervous System. Sleep, digestion, elimination, all depend upon a good state of the Nervous System. If we give in to worry, we create a vicious circle, for it tends to take away our sleep and impair our digestion, through running our nervous energy to waste; the consequence being that our ability to sleep, and digest our food, etc., becomes still further impaired. Our condition then goes from bad to worse; and it is all due to giving in to worry.

Most of us, I suppose, have known people of splendid type and high character who have become seriously ill and have finally died, all through worry, care, anxiety, which they failed to master. Disease is kept at bay in the case of the healthy by what are termed the powers of resistance. Worry tends to weaken these powers, and therefore, indirectly, may be the cause of many disorders.

Thank goodness, I am coming to the end of the negative aspect of my subject, so I will close this unpleasant part by pointing out that indulging in, or giving way to worry, is a form of negative thinking; and as we all know, this makes connections with, or attachments to, negative ills. If we think of evil, disaster and danger, and of ourselves as subject to them, then we make connections with them, and open channels through which they can flow to us.

Chapter Two

Don't Worry About Worry

It has been an unpleasant task, writing all this about the negative side of our subject. I should not have done so, of course, if it were not possible also for me to show a complete way of escape from it all, or rather a path of victory. Those who are given to worry, must however not add this to their worries, by being fearful about the effect of their worrying. As soon as they apply the remedy they will not only cease harming themselves, but they will also become healed of the past. "I will restore unto you the years which the locust hath eaten" is particularly true of worry.

When we cease to worry, and, instead, laugh with the carefree laughter of the sons of God, we are at once set free from the bugbear which has held us in the past.

The effect of worry is gradual. It must not be thought that because a person worries over something, he will fall a victim immediately to some fell disease. It is a tendency. It undermines his health. It lowers his powers of resistance. It is insidious. It is far reaching in its effects.

Nipping Worry in the Bud

Consider the case of a man with a big business worry. In the ordinary way he would spend a sleepless night, thinking, thinking, thinking, and still seeing no way out of his trouble. In the morning, he would rise feeling very seedy, less fit than usual to meet unusually exacting duties. Probably, his breakfast may disagree with him, and so he goes through his work both mentally and physically at a disadvantage, a mere bundle of nerves, to use a common, homely expression.

If, however, the same man were able to apply an antidote to his worry, how different the story would be. For a time, he would be sleepless, because he would be engaged in seeking and finding the antidote. But, having found it, he would pass into a joyful and peaceful sleep. In the morning, he would rise fit and well, ready for all emergencies. He would enjoy and digest his breakfast, after which he would proceed to his office, serene and confident. He might also wake up with an answer to his problem already in his mind; or it might come to him during his time of silence; or perhaps he would read an important phrase or verse. As a result of all this he would be able to meet his difficulty and problem in the best possible manner and be able to deal with it in the best possible way.

The Human Tendency to Worry

Until we learn how to apply the antidote, we are all liable to give way to worry, some much more than others. Some, of course, are of a naturally placid disposition, but the majority are not. But even the placid ones may worry, when faced by very great trouble. This brings us to our next point, which is, that those who worry are of two kinds: firstly, those who worry in spite of the fact that they have nothing about which to worry, and secondly, those who worry because they have some real trouble or problem.

In the case of the first named, worry is merely a habit, or weakness of character. Such may admit their foolishness by saying: "I know that I'm silly to worry, but I really can't help it. After all, you can't help your thoughts, can you?" By that they mean that it is impossible to control one's thoughts. Such people believe that everything *may* go wrong, and they fear that it *will* go wrong. If the postman comes with a letter, they worry as to the probable bad news that it may contain. If the postman does not bring a letter, then they worry because he has not brought one. If their husband is five minutes late home, they worry about it, wondering if he has been killed or locked up, or if he has eloped, or has committed murder. A man who sometimes used to come to see me, used to get up after a few minutes and take his departure, saying that he must get back home, or else his wife would think that he had been killed again. How many times he had been killed in imagination was past computation!

Needless Worrying

People who worry needlessly in this way do not receive much compassionate thought, but rather the reverse. For instance, people will say when speaking of such, "it would do them good if they had something really to worry about". This is almost as unkind as the remark of a man who said that he did not like to publish the fact that spiders are short-sighted, because it would be something more for people to worry about!

We all are agreed as to the folly of indulging in worry, when there is no real cause for worry; but what about the case of those who are in real trouble and difficulty? Such, of course, would have a very good excuse for giving way to worry, if it were not for the fact that worry never by any chance does good, but that actually it does a great deal of harm.

Having said far more about worry and its causes than I intended to, let us now consider together, some of the cures or antidotes.

Chapter Three

Thought Control

Much good may be done by practising thought control, especially in the case of worrying without due cause. There are plenty of people who have no real religious background, who yet refuse to worry. They have a philosophy which is, that as nothing is to be gained by worry, but only harm entailed, therefore they will not worry. They will take what steps are necessary in the face of every circumstance, as it arises, and then dismiss the matter from their mind. They realise that they must not give way to fear or panic, but that if they can remain calm and confident a way out of their difficulty will be found.

Such people are not sensitive. If something disturbing happens, they do their best in the circumstances and leave it at that. They do not lose any sleep over it. They have done their best, and as worrying over it would do no good, why worry!

If something upsetting happens, such as receiving a bad treatment at the hands of someone else; they do not spend sleepless nights over it, but they defend themselves and their feelings by rigorously pitying the one who has hurt them. He is a poor fool who is so ignorant he knows no better, etc. By so doing they prevent self-pity and so they are able to sleep and avoid worry, because they maintain the attitude that they are all right and that the other fellow is a fool. I do not, of course, suggest that our readers should follow such an example. It is only mentioned in order to show that people who are not sensitive and who have no knowledge of Truth, are yet able to face up to life's experiences by avoiding worry, through cultivating a thick-skinned insensitivity.

The Troubles of Sensitive People

But how different is the case of those who are sensitive! I knew a large draper once, who had a row of shops. He was practically interested in his business and made it his duty to investigate any complaint that a customer might make. He said that if a complaint were made, such as a piece of faulty material, it used to upset him so much, he could not sleep at all the night after it, and very little the following night. He suffered so much in this way that he gave up business. He was a very good Christian man, but he had not learned how to overcome worry. The irritations of business were allowed to worry, or bite like fierce dogs, right into that part of him which should have been always in a state of holy calm. And so his peace was destroyed, he was robbed of his sleep, and his health lowered, by what, after all, were trivial things.

False Thinking Posing as Right Thinking

The popular idea of thought control and the overcoming of worry is, however, erroneous. The popular idea seems to be that we should never think of anything unpleasant, but that we should dodge mentally all thoughts relating to unpleasant things and think of nice things instead. It is at this point that popular psychology goes astray.

This is a travesty of right thinking. No true psychologist would entertain such an idea for a moment, but I am afraid that many well-meaning people practise it and think that what they're doing is right thinking. What it actually is is a subtle form of wrong thinking.

Of course, we all know that it is bad for anyone to wallow in a trough of low, evil or pessimistic thoughts, and that if he would think on a higher plane, it would be so much better for him. Thus, if a person thinks hellish thoughts, then how much better would it be if he were to train his mind to think Heavenly thoughts. St. Paul gives us a good example of this, in Philippians 4:8, he tells us:-

> "Whatsoever things are true, whatsoever things are honest, whatsoever things are just, whatsoever things are pure, whatsoever things are lovely, whatsoever things are of good report; if there be any virtue, and if there be any praise, think on these things".

But this is very different from avoiding in thought the duties and challenges of life. We all know the weakening effects of daydreaming. If a person, instead of getting up and grappling with life's difficulties and problems, lies in bed, dreaming that he is a millionaire, or the Prime Minister, or a champion motorist, or aviator, we know that, so far from rising above the rank and file, he will be lucky if he does not descend into the submerged tenth.

Well, this pseudo right thinking, so-called, is a form of daydreaming. It avoids the challenge of life, it dodges the things which are disliked, but which ought to be faced and dealt with, and dreams instead happy futile dreams, which have no relation to our practical life here on earth.

We all know how dilatoriness, procrastination, and failure to make a decision weaken and destroy the character. Willpower becomes less and less, and a state of instability and even neurasthenia may result.

Thinking Through

True right thinking is thinking through. Instead of running away from a thought of an unpleasant duty, we think through it and see it completed. This act of thinking through to victory, first, in our mind's eyes, enables us to face up to our duty or task, and make a success of it.

If we face boldly, in our thoughts, all our troubles and difficulties (including the things which we would prefer to run away from), and overcome them, seeing ourselves victorious and successful, then we turn what would otherwise be worries into preparations for success in our outward affairs. The practice of such right thinking braces our will, increases our determination, and strengthens our character, so that nothing can worry us, because we have become too strong to be worried, and because we know that we are going to overcome and be victorious.

While true right thinking is very helpful, especially in overcoming the habit of worrying over trifles, and in meeting the ordinary troubles and difficulties of life, yet something else is needed when we meet with great trials, griefs, disappointments and experiences.

Psychology can deal only with thoughts and ideas, and the right use and control of these, of course, are very necessary, and must not be avoided or neglected. But, in addition to all this, we need something that is deeper and more fundamental. We have to get down to cause rather than to continue to deal with the effects, merely.

And this brings us to the one remedy and true antidote for all worry, care, fear, anxiety and trouble.

Chapter Four

The Antidote

It has been said that "the greatest antidote for worry is Religious Faith". Psychology very often proves ineffective in the face of great and real trouble, especially if there is no religious background, or what we would term a foundation of truth. I would go farther by saying that the antidote for worry is knowledge of truth, which is an understanding of God, and a continual abiding in Him and in His peace.

People talk about Christian faith, and, when we hear that, we may jump to the conclusion that it means knowing God, and abiding in Him, realising that all is well. But what such people mean, very often, is not that at all. What they mean is, the dogmas of Christianity, the framework of Christian belief, and so on. This is a very different matter. Dogmas and creeds no matter how perfect they may be, both theologically and metaphysically, can never be an antidote for worry.

We see proofs of this on every hand. We see people who are perfect as regards theological beliefs, and who are most correct and orthodox in their views, who yet give way to worry. Indeed, it was because, when I was younger, I saw so many exemplary

Christians, almost killed by worry, that made me determined to find out a way by which this terrible destroyer of health and peace and happiness could be overcome.

We see, then, that being correct in one's religious beliefs, blameless in one's conduct, and a real sincere follower of orthodox Christian teaching, are not in themselves an antidote for worry.

Yet, when we come to think about it, we see that true religion should cure us of worry. A worrying Christian is a contradiction of terms. If he really trusts in God, then he cannot worry. It was because of this that it has been said that the best antidote of worry is religious faith.

Our Lord said "if you would continue in my word... ye shall know the Truth, and the Truth shall make you free".

What did Jesus mean by this? Did he mean that we would understand theological truth, intellectually, and that through so doing we should be set free?

No, because those who are good theologians are as much given to worry as anyone else.

Did Jesus mean that we could study his teachings like a book of science, and gain certain information like a chemical formula, which would make us free?

No, because spiritual truths can only be spiritually discerned; while the carnal or sense mind regards spiritual truths as foolishness.

What Jesus said was "if ye *remain* in my word". This, according to Weymouth, is the literal meaning. Before we can *know* the Truth, we have to enter into It. Then, when we have entered into It we can abide in It; and because we abide in It, we are made free.

Until we enter into Truth, it is merely an intellectual concept to us. It has no power in our life: it cannot make us free.

So long as a man merely believes that he is a son of God, he simply holds an intellectual belief on the matter. This, of course, cannot free him from the worry habit: neither can it prevent negative thoughts from "worrying" themselves into his consciousness.

But when a man KNOWS that he is a son of God, he enters into freedom. He knows the Truth, and the Truth makes him free.

When we enter into Truth, we pass beyond the realm of ideas, thoughts and beliefs to the underlying Principle of Life.

Behind and beyond the surface of life, and behind and beyond all thoughts, there is, forever present, the perfect, Divine Principle of Life, which is the Cause or Essence of all life.

What is termed "realisation" is an expansion of consciousness in which we pass from effect to Cause, finding ourselves one with the Essence or Perfect Divine Principle. This is what is meant by KNOWING the Truth. The object of our Lord's teaching was that men should know the Truth, even as He knew it. Thus was He the first born of many brethren.

But, it may be argued, this is a state of attainment which few people can ever reach, why speak about it when dealing with worry? In the first place, it is easier of attainment than is generally thought possible; while, in the second place, it is the antidote, not only of worry, but of every human ill; and finally, it is by holding the possibility of attainment before people that makes them aspire after, and finally to find and enter into Truth.

The things which may cause anxiety and a state of worry today, are the very things which, if dealt with in a Truth way, will bring the seeker into a state of Realisation of Divine union, tomorrow. The things which may seem to be the greatest hindrance now, will prove to be the very thing which will bring the seeker into the Kingdom of Interior Harmony, in the near future.

If we concentrate upon getting rid of worry, only, then, after all, we are only dealing with things and effects. If, however, we enter into Truth, realising that we are one with the Interior Harmony Itself, then we are at the Source or Cause.

As we say in one of our Simple Talks series:

"This teaching does not deal with effects, but with causes: not with outward form, but with the inner power that produces all things."

Results cannot be brought about by dealing with effects, but only through realising our at-oneness with That which produces all things.

When we realise the Truth all our worries vanish. That is to say, we find God and abide in the Peace of God, after which, nothing else matters. Therefore, we do not worry, although there may be much in our life about which we might worry.

Behold I make All Things New

But there is more in it than this, because if we find the Peace of God, and abide in it, then peace and order tend to manifest in our life. When we get to the Source of all things, we are at that point that is spoken of in the Bible as "the beginning", which means, before the disorders from which mankind suffers arose. Through so doing, our life is built up anew after the Divine pattern, according to the Interior Harmony and Perfection.

A great deal of worry, with many people, is due to a belief that everything will go wrong if they personally do not prevent it. Such people cannot even let the world go round of itself, they are unconsciously trying to push it round. Consequently, they never rest. Even when they're asleep their body is not relaxed. To such I have to say: relax, let go, let the earth go round of itself, and carry you with it. When you lie down, do so, as though you would fall through the floor, instead of trying to hold the earth up by your tenseness.

Such people are in a state of continual worry and apprehension, because they fear that some disaster may come to them or their loved ones at any moment. They argue that because disaster comes to other people, many of them good Christians, therefore it may come to them.

Here, of course, one can advise certain psychological helps, but the only antidote or real preventative is to realise the Truth. Psychological methods may help one to keep his mind off such fears, and thus prevent them from becoming an obsession, but it is only the knowing of Truth that can give protection against possible evil and disaster.

The nearer we get to God the less striving there is, and the more there is accomplished; for God appears to do nothing, and yet does everything. What is termed the Adamic curse of strain, effort, toil, struggle, and opposing forces, duality, pairs of opposites etc., is overcome when we find God, and realise His harmony, order, completeness, self-sufficiency and self-contained self-renewing- from-within-nature.

St John illustrates this in his story of the disciples toiling with their fishing all night and yet catching nothing. Then the Lord comes and tells them to cast their net on the right side of the ship; whereupon they catch so many fish, it becomes impossible for them to draw their net. When we cease dealing with effects and turn instead to the One Source of all phenomena and form, then we become one with the Power that creates all things and find ourselves to be included in it. But, we do not reach this state by self-assertion, but only through complete surrender and great humbleness. This is one of the great paradoxes of the spiritual life.

Meeting Difficult Experiences

When we meet with a very upsetting experience, or receive disturbing news, we are tempted sorely to worry. All kinds of evil suggestions come to us, which, if allowed to do so, would destroy our peace by boring their way into our mental and spiritual stronghold like dogs worrying a sheep. At such times it is useless "to fight against worry", what we have to do is to apply the antidote, viz., to find God's peace.

We can never overcome an evil habit by fighting it, but only by doing something that is its very opposite. In this case, instead of worrying, we turn to God, and do not cease until we can abide quietly in His peace. If we find, and abide in God's peace, then the whole experience becomes healed, and a Divine adjustment is brought about. Psychology may prevent us from worrying over trifles and make us strong to face up to life's difficulties, but only realising the Truth and abiding in God's peace can heal the whole situation.

When faced by a situation or experience which we dread very much, we may at first pray frantically about it. We may pray desperately that this thing may come to pass, or that some other thing may not come to pass. If this is the best we can do in the way of prayer, then we should keep on with it; for any prayer is better than no prayer, and the Spirit helps our infirmities and teaches us how to pray.

But with more understanding, we pray only that the Divine Will may be done, and we express our willingness to go wherever God may want to lead us no matter what it may entail.

When we surrender in this way we enter into peace. When we surrender in this way it becomes possible for the Lord to heal the whole situation, thus bringing about a Divine adjustment, through what is termed mystical action in inaction.

The Way of Surrender

If we were to try to put things right by forming strong mental concepts of what we might think would be the best thing for us and insisting by our vehemence that they should come into manifestation, then we should only be using the human mind and would never know God's peace. But, when we know God's peace, through surrendering to His will, a Divine adjustment becomes possible, and this is far, far better than anything that we could plan or wish for ourselves. In fact, the comparison is absurd, for they are contradictions - the one is Divine harmony, while the other is human disharmony, or, at best, an imitation of the Divine harmony. The one is the house built upon a rock, while the other is the house built upon the sand.

A Poor Man Finds Truth

There was once a poor Christian man who fell out of work and suffered great mental anguish because he could not feed his children. When he was almost in despair, he read 1 Timothy 5,8. Such a text, so one would think, would have increased his anguish, but it had the reverse effect. He argued to himself that if one who did not provide for his children was worse than an infidel, then if God did not feed him, who was one of God's children, God would be worse than an infidel, which, as Euclid would have said, was absurd. Immediately, this man realised the truth that because he was a child of God, then his Heavenly Father was bound to feed him and provide for him. And so he entered into God's peace, through trusting implicitly in His love and care. He did not wait until he got employment before doing so - which is the human way of dealing with such things - but he trusted on the spot, and so entered into God's peace. The result, of course, was that he obtained work, and both he and his children were fed and provided for.

The human way is to expect the trouble to be taken away first, then after that to trust and cease to worry.

The Divine way is to trust in God and to find His peace, first. After which the healing of the whole situation follows, as day follows night.

The Value of the Psalms

Some of the Psalms are of the greatest help. Critics say that religion is merely so much "dope". Meaning by this that it is a drug like opium, which makes us dream pleasant dreams; but, at the same time, also unfits us for facing up to the realities of life. There is a travesty of religion which consists of daydreaming of the Better Land and indulging in sentimental emotions. This, of course, is both weakening and destructive, and must be avoided at all costs. It is a pathological state, or may lead to such a condition.

The use of the Psalms, on the contrary, is both positive and strengthening. It does not relegate good to a future time but brings it into the present moment. It does not dream dreams while duties and responsibilities call, neither does it "fiddle while Rome is burning". Instead, it faces the problem, the fear, or the worry, or the impending disaster, and brings Truth in opposition to it. There is no evasion: the Truth is brought squarely up against the trouble. We do not fight the fear and worry, but we bring against them, as an antidote, or neutralising force, the power of Truth, as given in the promises of God, as contained in the Psalms. Some Psalms are much more helpful than others. Also, one Psalm may be helpful to us in one situation, while, at another time, another one may meet our need.

Last night I turned to the 121st Psalm. I noticed the marginal version, and so for the first time the true meaning and *motif* of the Psalm. A very free rendering might be something like this.

> Shall I raise my eyes to the mountains?
> Is it from them that I receive my help?
> No, my help cometh from the Lord,
> Who created both the Heavens and the earth.

The argument is a sound metaphysical one. Shall I look to things and to effect? Is it from these that help can come? No,

I look to the Source and Essence, to the One Creative Power and Intelligence who creates all things.

By this sharp contrast the soul is turned from contemplating things to the contemplation of the One Supreme Power and Reality. Then the Psalm proceeds:

> "He will not suffer thy foot to be moved:
> He that keepeth thee will not slumber".

We may be facing a crisis in our life; even the very ground may appear to be crumbling from beneath our feet: our whole world may seem to be crashing into ruins; but, in the face of it all, comes God's unfailing promise: "he will not suffer thy foot to be moved: he that keepeth thee will not slumber".

Again, the Psalm proceeds:

> "Behold, He that keepeth Israel,
> Shall neither slumber nor sleep".

The Israel of God means all who love and revere the LORD; that is, all God's children at all times and in all ages. Here is the promise - ceaselessly, by night and day, always, every moment of our existence, He who loves us and cares for us, and Who protects us as part of Himself, He will never allow our foot to be moved.

But, God's love is shown to be greater even than this, for the Psalm goes on to say:

> The Lord is thy Keeper;
> The Lord is thy shade
> Upon thy right hand.

In a hot and weary land, where the sun scorches and withers - and this is a symbol of the wilderness of this world and the temporal life - under such conditions, the Lord is our shade. Through trust in Him we are protected from the destruction that comes to those whose life is not rooted in God.

And so the Psalm proceeds; and, as we read and ponder, we glide into God's peace. No matter what may happen, we are not troubled, for "He will not suffer our foot to be moved".

Through abiding in the realisation of this great truth, and through letting it soak into us, so that we become thoroughly impregnated with it, we are able to meet our difficulty, trouble, or fear, with courage and fortitude. Also, in addition, we find that a Divine adjustment is brought about which is far better and harmonious than anything that we could have planned for ourselves.

Replacing a Habit of Worry with a Habit of Abiding in God's Peace

But we must not wait until we are in trouble before making use of the Psalms in this way, for if we do so we may find ourselves so unskilled in the art of finding God's peace, that we are unable to overcome our agitation and thus remain a victim to worry. If we would be able to find God in time of trouble, or when we are worried, we must make a practice of finding Him when things are going smoothly with us. Indeed, there is a great secret here. There are times when it is very easy to find God's peace, and when it is possible to become conscious of Infinite love and Divine blessing pressing upon us.

If, at such times, we neglect to see God and to commune with Him, thinking that it does not matter, because everything is so harmonious, we are indeed foolish. If we act in this way, then our time of harmony will turn out to be only "a lull before a storm". But, on the other hand, if we make the most of the opportunity, by entering into and abiding in God's peace, allowing ourselves to be thrilled with the blessings which are pressing upon us, then we find that great joy and harmony come into our life.

God's Sustaining Grace
Thy love enfolds me, Thy power upholds me,
And Thy wisdom guides me.

Part 2: Release From Fear

Hamblin Vision Publishing

Chapter Five

Overcoming Fear

*Instead of fighting life, I love it;
and because of this life is friendly to me.*

When we overcome our fear, the thing that we fear ceases to have power over us.

Most people are the victims of fear. Some are kept back, and consequently make no progress in life, because of a hidden fear. Unconsciously, they may fear something - it may be responsibility, or meeting people, or taking the initiative - and because of this they avoid opportunities which, if seized, might lead to a much better and harmonious life. Unconsciously, because of some hidden fear, they constantly work against their own advantage.

Others may fear disease, sickness, ill health. They look with dread to the future, because it may bring them suffering and pain. Every time they hear that one of their friends or acquaintances is ill, or suffering from disease, they become filled with apprehension and misgiving.

Others fear that poverty, disgrace, disaster may come to them. What guarantee have they that they will not descend from affluence to the gutter? What is to become of them in their old age? Visions of the workhouse, with all its horrors, flit before their mind's eye. They are filled with dark forebodings for what the future may have in store for them.

Others, again, fear they know not what. Even the postman's knock fills them with nameless fear, so that they hardly dare go to the door. Yet others are the victims of waves of fear which sweep down upon them and prostrate them for days at a time.

I am able to describe the symptoms because I myself have suffered in this way. I have had to find my own way out, but I am telling others how it is done in order that they too may work out their own salvation.

Fear is due to the acceptance of suggestion. There is nothing to fear, really. It is through accepting suggestions of evil that we fear, and it is because we fear that it becomes possible for evil happenings to come to pass. The overcoming of fear means the overcoming of the thing that we fear therefore, the way of liberty is found only through the overcoming of fear.

In some cases, fear can be overcome by denying its power, and affirming the truth of being. For instance, fear may be met and overcome by facing it and stating the following:

> There is nothing in all the Universe that can make me afraid, because I am upheld by all the Divine forces of harmony and order.

If this is persevered with, gradually a realisation comes to the soul that all is well, and that one is upheld by benign and friendly powers, so that no evil can assail. It is of the greatest possible help if one really believes that inwardly and truly one is a spiritual being, forever loved and cared for by Infinite Being; but, even if one cannot do this, this method will be found effective by many.

Another way is to make friends with the threatened experience, or the thing which we do not like. So long as we are antagonistic to an experience it has power to hurt us. But as soon as we bless it, and make friends with it, and are willing to go all the way with it, it ceases to have any power to hurt us. This is why the greatest teacher of all said that we should agree with our adversary, and resist not evil, and that if a man should compel us to go a mile, we should be willing to go two miles. All this means that we should agree with and make friends with the experience which we fear and dislike, for then it no longer has any power over us.

CHAPTER SIX

The Inward Power

Withdrawing from the outer to the Inner I take my stand, in the Inward Power, which controls all things, and become Master of myself and of circumstances.

The previous chapter, when it appeared in the public press, aroused widespread interest. I only hope that many of those who read it may put its suggestions into practice, for if they do so, perseveringly, they will certainly make progress towards the overcoming of their fears. It is probable, however, that many will not try to do so, because the remedy is such a simple one. In this they are not alone, indeed they are in illustrious company, for no less a person than Naaman, the great captain over all the armies of the King of Syria, acted in a similar way. When he was told that if he would wash in the Jordan seven times, his leprosy would be healed, he flew into a rage and said: "Are not Abana and Pharpar, rivers of Damascus, better than all the waters of Israel? May I not wash in them and be clean?" However, in his case, his servants, being wiser than he (as sometimes happens), persuaded Naaman to obey the prophet's instructions, so that after all he did bathe seven times in the river Jordan and was made whole.

Most people will believe in a method of treatment if it is mysterious, or complicated, or very expensive, but will have nothing to do with a method that, while it may be more effective, has the disadvantage of being simple, not at all mysterious, and is offered free. Said the prophet:

> "Wherefore do you spend money for that which is not bread, and your labour for that which satisfieth not? Ho, everyone that thirsteth, come ye to the waters, and he that hath no money; come ye, buy and eat, yea, come, buy wine and milk, without money and without price".

The greatest things can never be bought with money. Those who have the greatest gifts to offer do not try to sell or barter them, but give them freely, without money and without price. Truth can never be sold. Those who try to sell it find that they have no truth to sell, while those who purchase find that what they have bought contains no treasure.

Some people think that if they can only discover some remarkable book or some wonderful treatment that emanates from someone "who is so clever", their troubles will then be at an end. This is a vain hope, for he who suffers from fear cannot be cured by others, he can be cured only by himself.

It has been said that a man who is his own lawyer has a fool for a client. This, while it may be true of the law, certainly does not apply to the overcoming of fear. Each victim has to work out his own salvation. This is really the beginning of the path of deliverance, viz. to recognise the fact that no one can help, and that if you are to be delivered you must win your way through to victory entirely off your own bat.

"Physician, heal thyself". Each one has to be his own physician, his own healer, his own deliverer, and to heal and deliver himself.

The first step, then, is to acknowledge the fact that we must depend upon no one else. Immediately we lean on others, down we go. We have to build up on a sure foundation of Inward Power and be master of our fate and captain of our soul. This Inward Power, however, is not our own ego power, but is the Power of the Indwelling God.

One of the secrets of all overcoming, be it of habit, sin, weakness, fear, sickness, poverty, is the realisation of the power within. "Greater is He that is in you than he that is in the world". In other words, the power within is greater than anything that is opposed to us.

CHAPTER SEVEN

The Power of the Infinite

Within you is the power. Not the feeble power of the finite personality, but the Infinite Power that sustains all things.

In the previous chapter it was shown that each one must overcome his own fear, for no one can overcome fear on behalf of another; each must win the victory for himself. It was also pointed out that there is a power within us which is greater than any difficulty or fearful or dreaded experience that can oppose us.

Many people are ready to admit that there is a power that is greater than circumstances, but comparatively few realise that this power is present within themselves. **"Within you is the Power"** conveys nothing to the majority, yet thousands of quite ordinary people have had their life transformed through realising the truth of it, as applying personally to them. So long as we think of ourselves as separate units, outside the Power of the Infinite, and at the mercy of unknown forces of evil, we remain helpless and the prey of waves of fear and apprehension.

But when we realise that the Power of the Infinite is within us, then the things which hitherto have affrighted and tortured us cease to have dominion over us.

We, however, have to avoid thinking that *we* are the power that is infinite, for to do so inflates the personal ego, so that it becomes a kind of Humpty Dumpty, who, as we all know, was a very fine fellow until he fell off the wall. If we indulge in such self-suggestions as: "I am Spirit", or "I am Power", we blow ourselves up like a toy balloon, which the first sharp experience that we meet punctures, with direful and humiliating results.

On the other hand, if we realise that while of ourselves we can do nothing, yet the Divine Power within us is greater than anything that comes against us then, no matter how fearsome the experience which we have to meet, we know that it is eternally true that "greater is He that is in you than he that is in the world". When we reach this stage, we not only rise superior to our fears, but we are also able to overcome our difficulties, and become conquerors in the battle of life.

Life can only beat us when it gets us down. We cannot be conquered if we refuse to be conquered, and will call upon the Inward Power, acknowledging that it *is* within us, and that it is greater than any difficulty. If we maintain the victorious attitude at all times, then life's difficulties or evils, instead of dominating us, flee away. Life itself may seem to us to be an oppressive tyrant, from whom we cannot escape; yet, when we realise, acknowledge and depend upon the power within, life ceases to be a tyrant, and instead, fawns at our feet. If, in the face of some overwhelming experience, we rise up in the might, majesty, and power of the Indwelling Infinite Spirit, then our troubles, fears, and difficulties become dwarfed, in much the same way that trees and buildings become flattened out when viewed from the top of a high hill.

The waves of fear which come sweeping down upon the one who has not yet learned to overcome are merely waves of suggestion. If they are accepted, they become part of the life. If they are rejected, they return to their native nothingness.

How to meet and overcome these waves of suggestion of fear and evil forms the subject of the next chapter.

Chapter Eight

Self-Mastery

Taking my stand in Eternal Truth, evil suggestion is foiled, and slinks away.

In order to overcome fear, it is necessary to attain self-mastery.

The waves of fear, which are really waves of suggestion of evil, which rush down upon those who are victims of fear and panic, can be effectively countered and overcome. Such waves of suggestion have power only on their own plane. If they are accepted, and if we allow them to overwhelm us, then they become a great power in our life. But if we refuse to accept them, then they have no power over us.

A moment ago, I said that these waves of suggestion have power only on their own plane. They can, therefore, be rendered harmless if we take our stand on a higher plane. The moment that we do this the suggestion which, on its own plane, has great power is neutralised and reduced to a state of helplessness. An angry sea may be very hurtful if we are in its surf, but if we climb to the cliff above, its power and fury cannot affect us in any way. It is precisely the same with the overcoming of fear; we have to take our stand on a plane above that of the suggestions of evil which seek to dominate us.

If waves of suggestion of failure and poverty assail us, and are given way to, i.e., accepted, then failure and poverty may become part of our life. If, however, we refuse to accept the suggestion, but meet it with counter suggestions of an opposite character, then the suggested state of failure and poverty cannot materialise. It is equally true of any other suggested form of evil. As soon as we rise above it, it becomes helpless and harmless, as far as we are concerned.

But how can we take our stand on a higher plane it will be asked. In order to do this, we have to assert that which is forever true of us interiorly, meaning that we are Sons of God. Paul describes the true man as being the offspring of God; while John exclaimed: "Beloved, now are we the Sons of God".

In the face of a wave of fear, which really is a wave of suggestion, we can say something like the following:

> "As a child of God, I refuse to accept this suggestion. Because I am a child of God, none of these suggested evils can affect me".

Of course, the great battle for mastery is not to be won easily. At first the fight is fast and furious, and it is found difficult to ally ourselves with the interior man who is the Son or Child of God, and to maintain our attitude. But, if we persevere, refusing to give way, or to shift our ground, then the assaults of evil suggestion become weakened, and we enter into a victorious and peaceful state of mind. Every time that we win the battle in this way, we make it easier for us to overcome the next conflict. Gradually, we gain the ascendancy, and become so strong and poised that these suggestions of fear and evil have no longer any dominion over us.

I have now shown you the way by which you can overcome every weakness - always by allying yourself with the higher interior Man/Woman, who is a child of God - and it remains for you to win your way to victory and freedom. Some readers have written offering me money for "treatment". I have explained to them that I have no treatment, and that I am not a practitioner. The secret of overcoming is being given in these simple chapters, and it remains for the reader to apply the truth that is imparted.

Chapter Nine

Doing the Things We Fear

Relying on the Inward Power, I do the thing that I fear to do, and choose the most difficult path in life. In so doing, I enter into freedom.

In this chapter the subject that I shall deal with is *"calling the bluff"*. In one sense, life is continually trying to bluff us. Life is always trying to frighten us with some bogey or other. Deep down in the mind of most of us is something that we fear. We all know how that heroes who are so fearless in battle, or exploration, or other daring hazards, often fear a woman, or making a speech, or going into a draper's shop. What most wage earners fear is unemployment. Others, again, fear publicity; they are self-conscious, afraid of people looking at them. Others may fear interviews. I once knew a man who fainted if he saw a spider! We may not be as bad as that, but most of us fear something. Already, in previous chapters, I have described various methods of overcoming fear, principally of the nameless variety. Here follows a method that we all must employ if we are to overcome our pet fear or fears, once and for all.

Briefly, it consists in "calling the bluff" of the thing that we fear, by doing it. Some reader may at once say: "But that is impossible". Well, so long as he says it is impossible, it will remain impossible to him. But actually, it is not impossible. "All things are possible to him that believeth". Which means: all things are possible if we believe them to be possible. We have only to "call the bluff" in order to prove not only that to do what we fear is possible, but, also, that it is ridiculously easy.

What we have to do, then, is to do the thing that we most dread to do. If we do this, then we find that it has been all bluff, and that we actually can do the thing which we thought was impossible and do it easily. If you are self-conscious, then go and put yourself right in the front where you are stared at by the people you are afraid of. If you do this – I wonder if you will? – you will soon find your self-consciousness to be a thing of the past, and a thing to be laughed at. The thing that we fear can dominate us only so long as we shrink from it. Immediately we face it, and do so in its most aggravated form, it has no longer any power over us. This only proves what I said just now, that life is continually bluffing us, and that there is nothing to fear, whatever. As soon as we face up to the thing that we fear, it dissolves away.

It is the same with our tasks and difficulties. If we fear them, they tower above us, and life becomes too much for us. But if we choose the most difficult of our tasks *and do it*, we soon find ourselves on top of life, instead of overwhelmed by it.

Would you be on top of life, and be free, and have everything in order? Then call the bluff on all your fears, and do your most difficult tasks first, and always choose the most difficult course in life. To do this is to tread the Path of Victory. This is gloriously possible, for, *"Greater is He that is in you than he that is in the world"*.

Chapter Ten

Making Friends With Life

Perfect love casteth out fear.

St. John

I have just spoken of calling the bluff, or doing the thing we fear most to do, for by so doing we can win through to a measure of freedom from fear; but without so doing we must inevitably remain in bondage forever.

There is, however, one other thing about which I must speak, which is of very great importance.

In order to overcome fear of life, we must become friendly towards it. A very wise and understanding man once said: "Perfect love casteth out fear, for fear hath torments". There was never a truer word spoken. When we become friendly towards life, and every experience and every creature, we discover that there is nothing to fear, for we live in a friendly universe, and, as Edward Carpenter said, in his prose poem *Towards Democracy*: "All the divine forces hasten to minister to our eternal joy".

As soon as we can "love", or become friendly with, an experience, then that experience can no longer hurt us, but can only bless us, and minister to our joy.

It is possible to become so attuned to the universe that we are in friendly relationship with every atom in it. Then we find that, instead of things and events working against us, they actually work for us, seeking to bring us into a state of perpetual joy and harmony.

Consequently, we are never afraid of any experience that life can bring to us, for we know that a friendly universe is striving to bring us to our highest good, to lead us to a higher stage of good, and to a greater measure of good than ever possible to us before.

One of old said: *"All things work together for good, to them that love God"*. Again, one greater bids us to love God with all our strength, and our neighbour as ourselves. All this means that we should become friendly with the whole universe, and with life and all its experiences, and of course with the one origin of all good, order and harmony. If we do this, we find the harmonious life.

The teaching of Jesus is quite simple. It means that if we follow it, we become friendly with life, and live in friendly relationship with all its experiences, and with all our fellow creatures. Finally, we find the harmonious life, called the Kingdom of Heaven. This merely means that we come into harmony with, and in a state of union with the one centre and source of all harmony and order.

Life is a symphony that is always being played. Love is the conductor, and He beats the time. If we play our part according to the score, and come in on the right beat, and on the right note, then our life forms part of the glorious symphony of life, and life is indeed glorious.

Naturally, all fear passes away, for what can life do to us, but bring us to ever-increasing good, and to our eternal joy?

The eternal harmony and order are forever present. It is for us to bring ourselves into accord and correspondence with them. The universe and its laws cannot be altered, either to please or help us: neither would it be necessary or advisable so to do. It is we who have to be brought into correspondence with them. Then we find that there is nothing to fear, because we have entered into the interior harmony of the universe, through being attuned to it by love.

Chapter Eleven

Putting It into Practice

Not by might, nor by power, but by my spirit, sayeth the Lord of hosts.

Freedom from fear, and liberation from the bondage to which our fears have shackled us, is attained in a twofold way. Not by one method can we attain to freedom, but only by the two being assiduously employed. The first method is subjective. The second method is objective. The first consists in re-educating the mind and bringing forth the power of the spirit. The second consists in dealing with practical affairs, or, in other words, putting into practice the knowledge that we possess.

It is useless, and even harmful, to do the subjective work, and then to refuse to carry it out in everyday life. On the other hand, it is very difficult, if not impossible, to work objectively without the use of interior powers. Both methods are necessary, and, if they are persevered with, much may be achieved.

In the first chapter I described a simple method of denial and affirmation. In the face of fear, you were taught boldly to declare that there is nothing in all the universe to make you afraid. The subconscious mind has to be treated like a child. If a child is afraid of something, you first tell her that there is nothing of which to be afraid, that it is only her fancy, and so on. After this denial you proceed to the positive affirmation of what is true. Similar methods have to be employed when dealing with the subconscious mind. First, the cause for any fear is denied. In the face of fearful happenings, it may seem foolish to deny that there is anything of which to be afraid. But it is not foolish, really. It is a law of life that when fear is completely removed nothing can hurt us. Of the prophet Daniel it was said that when he was thrust into the lion's den the Lord shut the mouths of the beasts, so that they could not hurt him. This can be explained in this way, that Daniel's trust in God was so great he was completely delivered from all fear, and because of this the lions could not touch him. We all know that a dog who will attack one who is afraid of him will not attempt to hurt one who is entirely fearless. It is said that initiates and adepts in India go and sit in the jungle amidst wild beasts, and they're not molested, simply because they are entirely devoid of fear.

Shadrach, Meshach, and Abed-nego possessed such a faith and trust in God that they were not afraid to face the fiery furnace. Because of that absolute trust in a Higher Power, they were entirely free from fear so that no fire could touch them. Indians at the present day, after being suitably prepared, by religious purification, walk barefoot through burning embers, the heat of which is so fierce that it melts the varnish on chairs or seats placed near the fire. Yet they suffer no harm, not even the slightest blister being raised.

The total overcoming of fear means the complete overcoming of the thing that we fear. If fear is fully overcome, then the thing of which we are afraid cannot hurt us.

First of all, then, we have to overcome fear, inwardly or subjectively. Paradoxically, we have to realise inwardly that, actually, there is nothing to fear, because nothing can hurt us, although at the same time nothing can hurt us because we are unafraid. This is really a spiritual (not spiritualistic) achievement; It is a state of soul; it is an attainment to Divine knowledge and understanding.

Ordinarily, we can see only the thing that causes our fear, so that to realise anything different seems quite impossible. In order to realise the truth, the spiritual mind has to be aroused and caused to function. Statements of truth, repeated and impressed upon this mind tend to awaken the mind, so that it can understand interiorly, or realise the truth of the statement of Truth.

It is not possible to describe what "realisation" means. It can be experienced, but never described. All that I can say is that it is a state of awareness by the soul. The soul, through the functioning of the Spiritual or Super-conscious mind, is able to know and understand the great secret and truth which the greatest intellect is quite incapable of grasping.

The object of such a statement as that given in the first chapter:

> There is nothing in all the Universe that can make me afraid, because I am upheld by all the Divine forces of harmony and order.

...is to impress this truth upon the mind to such a degree that the spiritual mind begins to function in sympathy. Then a state of illumination comes to the soul, and light comes in and disperses the natural darkness of our mind.

It is all a matter of vibration. The truth when uttered and reiterated has power - vibratory power. It sets forces in motion. It arouses things of a like vibration into activity. We are told that creation followed the spoken word of Elohim: "Let there be light: and there was light", and so on. Also at the tomb, Jesus spake in a loud voice: "Lazarus, come forth"; and he that was dead came forth. The walls of Jericho fell down as a result of horn blowing and shouting used in a way of which present-day science is ignorant.

If, then, we want to be freed from fear, we should state the real truth of the whole matter. The statement of truth we have given is a certain vibration. It speaks of things as they really are. Each one of us, actually and interiorly, is a spiritual being, rooted and grounded in the eternal, living his life in God. Each one of us is a son or child of God, forever loved and cared for, and upheld by Divine powers. *"The eternal God is our refuge, and underneath are the Everlasting Arms"*. In the light of all this, it is seen, at once, that our statement of truth is indeed a true one. Because it is eternally true, it is capable of arousing the spiritual mind and causing it to function. Because it is eternally true, it brings truth into manifestation in the form of order, harmony, and peace.

It is of a similar vibration to all other statements of Truth. For instance:

> The Lord is my Shepherd;
> I shall not want.

In this case the positive affirmation comes first, and the denial is put second; but generally, the denial is put first. For instance:

> Yea, though I walk through the valley of death,
> I will fear no evil.

This is the denial. Then follows the affirmation:

> For thou art with me;
> Thy rod and Thy staff they comfort me.

It is not generally realised that the object of the psalms is to produce a psychological effect. Their object is to arouse the spiritual mind – that stratum of mind that can think God's thoughts after Him, and understand Divine things and ultimate truth, - thus bringing about a state of realisation.

Just as the children of Israel caused the walls of Jericho to fall down through the occult use of vibratory forces, so also can we cause the walls of our fear phantoms to collapse through our statements of truth.

In the face of fear, then, we have to state the truth that there is nothing to fear, and that we are upheld by all the benign forces of the universe. This is the spirit of the twenty-third psalm, and of others like it. If we repeat and meditate upon these statements of truth, then our inward understanding opens, so that we *know* the truth, and then the truth that we *know* interiorly, and realise, makes us free

When waves of fear and panic come rushing down upon us, we may feel too agitated to do anything, except to give way to them. A chain of evil happenings opens up before our imagination, and we picture disaster upon disaster ahead of us. Yet, in the face of it all, we should sit down and quietly but firmly declare the truth.

> The Lord is my shepherd;
> I shall not want.

> I am a child of God, eternally loved and cared for, I am one of the offspring of God, and because of this it is fundamentally true of me that *"The Eternal God is my refuge, and underneath are the Everlasting Arms"*. This is the only truth about me, at all times. God alone can deliver and

protect me, and because I put my whole trust in Him, he is able to do for me exceeding abundantly above all I can ask or think.

Because I am a child of God, and because all the benign powers of the Universe are on my side, and behind me, pushing me forward to victory, no evil can come nigh me, and nothing can hurt nor destroy. For He gives His angels charge over me, and they keep me in all my ways, and they bear me up in their hands lest I dash my foot against a stone.

Nothing but good can come to me. All the Divine forces are on my side. Because I am friendly towards all the Universe, the Universe is friendly towards me, so that everything works together for good, and "all the Divine forces hasten to minister to my eternal joy."

The above is a form of positive affirmative prayer, which, if persevered with, will bring deliverance from fear, and peace to the mind.

My experience has been that we should never go to bed in a state of worry or fear; neither should we retire if we experience a feeling of impending evil. Before retiring, it is necessary that we should overcome fear, worry, apprehension, and so on, by persevering with our declaration and reiteration of truth, until the sense of release and peace comes to the mind and soul. Then, and not till then, are we fit to retire for the night.

By working mentally and spiritually in this way we not only overcome our fears, but we also dissipate or dissolve the thing that has been the cause of our distress.

Overcoming, however, in this way, is not enough. In the outward life of affairs, we must put our realisation into practical effect by doing the thing, which in the ordinary way we are afraid to do. If we are afraid to meet a certain difficult person, then we must go and see him, and boldly beard the lion in his den. If we are afraid of speaking or appearing in public, then we must do the very thing that we are afraid most to do. Power is given us to do that which may seem to be impossible. Then we find that it was not so difficult after all.

Chapter Twelve

In Tune with the Universe

When we realise that we are in tune with the Universe, and in a state of friendly relationship with every particle of it, we enter into peace, and all fear passes away.

But we cannot become attuned to the Universe in this way if we are not friendly towards it. The Universe is one complete whole, with God the centre, and we form a part of it, in much the same way that a cell is part of the human body. The Universe, also, is a living Universe, as sensitive as a plexus of nerves. If we act in an unfriendly way, we become an enemy of the Universe. We are out of harmony with its spirit. Through our unfriendly act, we become an alien, and, because of this, the whole of the Universe is against us.

When unfriendly and harmful microbes enter the human body, great armies of corpuscular defenders are marshalled against them. The whole of the body is in a state of enmity against the intruders, seeking to destroy them. In the same way, if we act in an unfriendly way towards the universe, then we are like the unfriendly microbes, and the whole body of the universe is against us.

If we act against the principle of life, then, instead of being an harmonious part of a perfect whole, we are a plague spot in the cosmic body; consequently, our end will be destruction, unless we change.

The underlying principle of life and the universe is love, i.e., co-operative goodwill. If we act selfishly, or hurt or harm any brother, or living creature, we act as an enemy of life; consequently, the whole universe is against us, because we are against it. All the troubles, disasters and calamities in the world are due to man working against the laws of the universe and the principles of his being. All the universe is against man because man is against the universe. One man's hand is against his brother's, also he preys upon the humbler creatures, and because of this he violates the laws of life, and becomes an enemy of the universe. Therefore, everything works against him, and will continue to do so until he becomes changed, so that he works with the law of co-operative goodwill, instead of in opposition to it.

The same thing applies to each individual life. So long as we act selfishly, or harm our brother, or entertain thoughts that are not those of love, goodwill, and co-operation, we remain out of harmony with life, and the whole universe is against us.

It must not be thought because the whole universe is antagonistic towards us, when we live and work against its laws, that life's intention, or the universe, is evil. Life and the universe are infinitely good. It is because man is out of harmony with it all that he becomes hurt. It is because he works "on his own", in opposition to the internal harmony of life and the universe that everything seems to be against him. Indeed, the more perfect, and good and loving life and the universe are, the worse off does man become in consequence, if he does not live in harmony with them. It is not through life and the universe being evil, or cruel, or unkind, or vindictive, that man is hurt, but it is their very goodness, and because they are based upon the law of love, that makes everything work against him. It is like a schoolboy refusing to do his sums according to the rules of arithmetic. No matter how he may try, the answer to his sums will always be wrong, so long as he persists in working against the laws governing arithmetic. If, however, he will acknowledge his error, and learn to work according to the rules of arithmetic, then he will obtain correct results.

Therefore, before we can say, truthfully, that the whole universe is behind us, and its benign powers upholding us and pushing us forward to ever increasing good, we must come into friendly relationship with it. This we can do, first, mentally, and in spirit, and then in actual deed and action.

If every day we spend a short time in declaring that we love everybody, then in our contact with people we find it easier to act, not only justly and humanely, but also in a brotherly way. Through the practise of this we gradually find our life transformed; for we find God everywhere, in every experience, and in every person we meet. We also realise that all the divine forces are on our side; and this is simply because we have come into friendly relationship with the universe.

In my book *Daily Meditations*, on the page for Thursday, you will find the following prayer benediction. The effect of using this is to make true in us that which we declare. But only if we try to act up to what we say. This is it:

> To all the world is my love extended,
> *"Dear people, everywhere, I love you all, I love you".*
> To all who have injured or wronged me; to all who have vexed or ruffled me:
> *"I love you, and forgive you, even as my Father forgiveth me.*
> *May you be blessed in the best of all ways.*
> *May you be filled with joy unspeakable".*

If we make use of the above, daily, we find many opportunities given us of acting according to its spirit. Some of these opportunities may be very difficult, very hard to bear, and also very perplexing. But, if we do the best we can to live up to our declaration, then strength is given us to do the difficult thing, and to love where once we would have hated, and be merciful where once we would have been hard.

It now becomes easy to understand the teaching of Jesus, which previously may have seemed hard and purposeless. When He tells us to love one another, and even to love our enemies; to love God with all our heart, and soul, and mind, and our neighbour as ourselves; to do good to those who persecute us, slander us, and ill-treat us, we see that it is simple common sense instruction, by the observance of which we can enter into harmony with life and the universe. It means more than this, for it brings us into freedom and liberation. It sets us free from the shackles of earth so that we cease being earthbound sons of mortality, becoming instead sons of God and eternity, enjoying the liberty of the Sons of God.

When we are willing to come into harmony with the universe, and when our prayer is that we may love all men, forgive all men, and help all men, and when our love extends to all creatures and all creation, then it becomes possible for us truthfully to say:

There is nothing in all the universe to make me afraid, for I am upheld by the divine forces of harmony and order.

CHAPTER THIRTEEN

Our Eternal Nature

The waters know their own, and draw
The brooks that spring in yonder height,
So flows the good with equal law,
Unto the soul of pure delight.

~ John Burroughs

In addition to all that has been said in the foregoing chapters about living in harmony with life's laws and the interior harmony of the universe, and affirming the power of the Indwelling God, something else is required. To become entirely free from fear, even of death itself, we need to realise our eternal nature. When we realise that we are one with that which changeth not, and that all the cosmic powers and forces are working together for our highest good and our eternal joy, we enter into the peace of God.

No such realisation can come to us as a result of intellectual striving, but only through the awakening of an inward understanding. It is interiorly that we are one with the eternal and unchanging, and it is interiorly that we can understand this sublime truth. It is incomprehensible to the intellect, but it can be understood and realised by the soul. The intellect can understand the outward man and the world of effect; but it is the soul that understands the inner man and the world of reality.

The effect of affirming the truth, and of thinking of ourselves as a spiritual being, living in a spiritual universe, governed by spiritual laws, and upheld, and sustained by spiritual powers... is to awaken within us the spiritual faculty of understanding and realising the truth, by direct knowing, and not by the intellect, and oftentimes in spite of it.

This inward faculty by which we know the truth about God, and the truth about ourselves as children of God, is really a very highly developed and spiritual intuition. By it we simply know. We do not know *how* we know, but we understand and enter into truths so great and wonderful that the intellect cannot grasp them.

Through this inward realisation we enter into peace, because we know that we are the offspring of God, forever upheld and sustained, and loved, and guided; and also, that the one desire of Heaven is to guide, bless, support, and raise us to itself. This, of course, is no intellectual belief or understanding, but an interior realisation, which cannot be described, although it can be experienced.

The object of prayer is to raise us to this super-conscious condition. All prayer is good, but affirmative prayer is the most effective. An affirmative prayer is one which states the truth about God, and the interior truth about ourselves. The 23rd Psalm is an affirmative prayer. It states the truth about God, as a loving shepherd working on our behalf, and the truth about ourselves, loved and cared for by the same good shepherd. It does not ask for any favours: it simply states that which is eternally true. The effect of using the 23rd Psalm, every day, is gradually to bring us into a state of realisation. There are other passages in the Bible equally effective, and there are also statements of Truth outside the Bible which are helpful also. Any poem, for instance, that is written from the Cosmic standpoint, is helpful if it is repeated, over and over again.

In my struggling days I used to pace for hours beneath the stars, repeating John Burroughs' noted hymn, of which a verse is reproduced at the head of this chapter. I used to repeat this verse until I reached a state of realisation and peace. Another verse also was very helpful. When "wound up" and too anxious, this verse would help me to let go, and to relax. It runs as follows:

> I stay my haste, I make delays,
> For what avails this eager pace!
> I stand amid the eternal ways,
> And what is mine shall know my face.

Through reciting this verse we are able to relax, to rest in *the eternal*, and to let all our care, anxiety and strain fall away from us, so that we are at peace.

The result of all this is to bring us to a state of inward understanding and awareness, in which we know that interiorly we are eternally spiritual beings, living our true life in God. We know that we are not the sport of fate, and that we do not have to chase after things, but that everything that we need is drawn to us. Instead of running after things, all the time being filled with anxious fears, and strain, and worry, we relax and let go, taking our stand in God and truth; and through so doing we attract the best things of life, so that they want to come to us.

We realise with the psalmist that so long as we maintain this attitude, which he describes in the 23rd psalm; and that so long as we live in the consciousness in which he was when he wrote it, that good only can come to us, and that we have nothing to fear.

> For Thou art with me,
> Thy rod and thy staff
> They comfort me.

and :

> Surely goodness and mercy
> shall follow me
> all the days of my life.

Part 3: Making Friends With a Friendly Universe

Hamblin Vision Publishing

CHAPTER FOURTEEN

Making Friends With a Friendly Universe

Only too often, alas, is it not true that we live miserable lives of separation and isolation, in which everything seems to be against us, simply because we are not friendly towards life?

Is it not true that we play a lone hand which is against everybody else, and against all the invisible forces of life, instead of working in co-operation with them?

As a natural consequence, all the universe seems to be against us. Yet this is the reverse of what is the true state of affairs. The universe, so far from being unfriendly towards us, is friendly indeed, but we, by our separatist, unfriendly attitude towards it, and towards life and our fellows, make everything appear to be against us.

Like the army recruit who, because he was out of step, thought that the whole company was out of step with the exception of himself, we also create a state of disorder through being in a state of disunity with life and the universe, and yet perversely imagine that life and the universe are at fault and not we, ourselves.

Let us Change our Attitude Towards Life

Life is friendly indeed. It is continually seeking to bring us into friendly unity with itself. Its order, harmony, beauty, joy and perfection are always present, awaiting and inviting our recognition. Yet, we go on with blind eyes and dark mind, unappreciative of the splendour that lies so close to hand.

But, although life's order and beauty are always present, awaiting our discovery, and also our recognition and acceptance, yet these things are not revealed to those who are not ready. The beauties of the reality are not exposed to the gaze of the uninitiated. This does not mean that the inner kingdom can be discovered only by the highly educated. Exterior education and surface culture have nothing to do with the matter at all. The preparation that is required is one of the heart.

> "When it (the heart) shall turn to the Lord, the veil shall be taken away".

When our heart is turned to love it becomes possible for the spirit of love, beauty, order and perfection to enter us, so that we are able to see and apprehend that beauty which is always present, but which although revealed unto babes (those who have been born into, and awakened by the spirit), is hidden from the wise and prudent, i.e. those who have exterior and intellectual understanding, but not the inner perception of the spirit.

Chapter Fifteen

The Open Door

When this understanding comes to us it is as though a door in our mind were opened. Suddenly, silently, and without any effort on our part, the veil is taken away, and we enter a new world of indescribable loveliness. Or, rather, for a brief space we see things as they are and enter into reality.

We enter into a world where everyone and every creature and everything is friendly to us. We are made welcome, and we become one of themselves, so to speak. Indeed, it is something more wonderful than this, for it is as though our spirit expanded and embraced all creation. Not only are we at one with every soul and every creature and every thing, and not only are the hills and the woods our friends, drawing nigh to our spirit, but it seems as though we, ourselves, are the one spirit present in all things. Time and space are effaced for the moment, and we are at the dawn of creation:

> "When the Morning Stars sang together, and all the sons of God shouted for joy".
>
> Job, Chapter 38, Verse 7

For a time, we walk on air, and every bush is ablaze with God, and for once our heart is at rest, and our soul satisfied. We have entered into the true world of inexpressible joy and delight; we have come at last into friendly relationship with the *whole* and are satisfied.

Gradually, we come back to our so-called normal consciousness, and probably the first thing that we have to deal with may rub us up the wrong way. There is always something which, because it is trying and difficult, keeps our balance, and makes us keep our feet on the earth, and also to stay our mind upon God in order that we may keep our mind serene and in God's peace.

But, in spite of the insistence of practical affairs, we have had our moments of extended vision, in which we have seen things as they really are; and because of this we *know* that the reality is infinite joy.

Expansion of Consciousness

What I am trying to explain is an expansion of consciousness in which one sees with the eyes of Christ and enters into a state of oneness with the divine heart of the universe, called by some the Cosmic Christ, or Universal Lord. It may come to anyone who lives the spiritual life, and who makes contact daily with his divine source. No training is necessary. It just comes when we are ready for it. It should never be forced, and it can never be found by strain and effort. When we least expect it, we glide out into eternity and know ourselves to be children of the eternal and one with *that which changeth not*. Then it makes us smile when we think of learned theologians giving lectures in which they discuss and explain why they hope that the soul is immortal, and that there probably is such a thing as eternal life. Such lectures of course do good and are helpful to people when at a certain stage, but, when we enter into truth, such explanations and theories, good though they may be, become unnecessary and superfluous.

Chapter Sixteen

Seeing God

Mysticism has been defined as "looking into Heaven with a ghostly eye", or seeing with the eye of the soul. Such a definition is rather misleading. It gives one an idea of peeping into a room. But the understanding which comes to the soul is very different from that. Instead of peeping into a place, the consciousness expands until it embraces the Whole, and love unites all in the one, in delightful unity. "Peeping into Heaven" still maintains the false idea of separateness, and also, the equally false idea of Heaven being an objective thing in itself. When we enter into Truth, the false idea of separateness falls away, and Heaven is found to be part of our expanded consciousness. In other words, it is an expression of the harmony that is in our own soul; and this harmony is due to the presence of the Spirit of God within us.

Seeing God, when we are Like God

St. John made a great discovery when he cried:

> "Behold what manner of love the Father hath bestowed upon us that we should be called the sons of God... Beloved, now are we the sons of God, and it doth not yet appear what we shall be, but we know that when He shall appear we shall be like Him".

We can see God everywhere only to the extent that God is in us. We are sons of God only to the extent that God dwells in us and changes us into his own likeness. To the extent that this is achieved, to that extent are we able to see God appearing everywhere around us. God is love, and, when we are indwelt by the spirit of love, we become love, and to the extent that we become love, and really love God and every person, creature and nature and circumstance, to that extent do we find the heart of the universe, which is love.

Seeing God Everywhere

Therefore, in order to see God we have to be filled with spirit. "Blessed are the pure in heart, for they shall see God". To the extent that we can love do we become like God who is love, and to the extent that we become like God, do we see God everywhere. "When he shall appear, we shall be like him"; and we might say with equal truth; when we are like him then we shall see him as he is.

There is one universal force behind everything, every being, and every circumstance. We find God revealing himself-herself to us in many different ways, usually at unexpected moments. Then, in the twinkling of an eye, we become changed, and everything becomes alive with God. Suddenly, we become conscious that we have touched the heart of the universe, and that we are one with all nature, all creation, all joys and sorrows, all people and creatures, all events and happenings – in fact all that makes up the *one complete whole*, which is God.

These times of enlightenment, when we touch the very heart of the universe, may come to us all. They are not the sole prerogative of a privileged few. At any time, any one of us may find himself looking beyond time, realising that he belongs to the eternal.

It is not when we seek these experiences that they come to us, for they come to us when we least expect them. Suddenly, the world becomes changed, and is revealed to us in inexpressible beauty, and with a strange luminosity. In a moment, or in the twinkling of an eye, as Paul puts it, we are changed, for the transformation takes place in us and not in our environment. Then it is that we see with the eyes of the Cosmic Christ, or Universal Lord, who puts his spirit in us, so that we see with his eyes, understand with his mind, and feel with his heart; and so we see God everywhere. How wonderful and glorious it all is!

As Mother Julian of Norwich puts it:

The Lord puts into our heart the desire for the thing that he wants to give us. In other words, the Lord first puts into our hearts a desire to see the Lord. Then, because we cannot do so of ourselves, he puts his Spirit in us, so that we can see with his eyes, and thus see him everywhere, for he is the only reality.

Chapter Seventeen

Knowing and Illusion

We should never strain after experiences, or seek to have Cosmic Consciousness, or anything of the sort. All that we need to pray for is more of the Divine Spirit. We have to seek the Kingdom of God first; then, whatever is necessary is added. If, however, we seek the other things first, we not only miss the genuine thing, but we may be deceived by false states of consciousness, and also, we fail to find the Kingdom. If, however, we pray for more of the Divine Spirit, then, through the Spirit entering into us, we see with the eyes of Christ, and thus discover everything.

Always we find God as the universal heart of love that is behind everything. Love is the key, always, as has so often been said. When we can love sufficiently it is as though a door opens within our heart and mind, and we glide out into the Eternal, so to speak, or into an expanded state of consciousness.

God has revealed himself to me, sometimes, when I have been in the woods, and little wild animals and birds have played around my feet. Suddenly, I have *known,* and I have entered into the *great peace* and have known myself to be one with all life; and it has seemed as though I have been the universal life itself. But this, of course, has not been so, really, but has been due to the Divine Spirit entering my soul, thus causing me to see and hear and feel in harmony with Itself. Of myself I can do nothing, of myself I am nothing, and without the Divine Spirit I have no life, not even existence, and not even a memory of an existence.

Perpetuating an Illusion

The separate self is an illusion, a mere shadow on the screen of time. If I affirm that I am anything, then all that I do is to perpetuate the illusion of the "self" of separation. In other words, it becomes impossible for me to enter the Kingdom. If, however, I admit that I am nothing, then it becomes possible for Christ to become all in all. Or, as I heard a vicar once say from the pulpit of a parish church, the Holy Spirit can enter us and possess us so completely as to become our real self.

This sudden opening up of the consciousness has also come at other times: in early spring mornings, in the hush of evening, at some funerals, and when faced by great difficulties. At such times the Divine Spirit has graciously come to me, so that, to a certain extent, I have seen with his eyes, have understood with his understanding, and have realised a wonderful oneness with all life, and with the whole universe and the order which upholds it. My first attempt at writing was inspired by a bowl of spring flowers which my wife had placed on my desk or table. What I wrote was afterwards published in a book form and known as *The Message of a Flower*. In it, I make an attempt to explain what I feel and know and understand whenever I look at a flower. At first it was only at times that I was taken out of my usual material consciousness into that expanded consciousness in which one realises his oneness with the archetypal world, but now whenever I look at simple (not exotic) flowers the transition takes place. Here is what I wrote thirty-six years ago:

> But it is not by simply gazing at the flowers and looking upon them merely as 'pretty things' that we can see into, and enter into, the heart of God. Flowers, if we are to read their message, must be understood spiritually. To look at a flower as a 'pretty thing' is one thing, and to see a flower as the workmanship of the Divine Master Craftsman, and to read in it a message of Divine Love, is something entirely different. We need not be poets or artists in order spiritually to understand flowers, for even the most matter-of-fact person can see God's face in a flower if he or she will only look and try to understand.
>
> How, then, shall we look in order that we may understand? First of all, we must learn to observe. Let us go up to the flower and examine it carefully and in detail. Notice the exquisite colouring, the delicate texture, the beauty of

form, the glorious workmanship. Let these sink into our mind. Now let us notice the simplicity, the purity, the innocence, the expression, and let these sink into our mind. Now let us gaze very earnestly at the flower and try to catch its spiritual radiations. As we continue to gaze at it, we feel its radiations being absorbed into our being. The flower changes, it becomes more ethereal, more beautiful, more spiritual, more transparent; it becomes luminous with heavenly light. Let us stand perfectly still and absorb the flower's spiritual beauty and radiance, for we are beginning to see not the physical flower, but its spiritual prototype instead. Now, led by the flower, our thoughts become more spiritual, and we realise that this beautiful ethereal blossom is a thought of God. If this beautiful emblem is a thought of God, what a beautiful mind God has, and if this lovely flower had its origin in God's heart what a heart of love He must have?

The Message of a Flower, by HT Hamblin

In these various ways one discovers the heart of the universe, which is God's heart of love. We have to love much, before we are admitted as one of the inner circle. If we are friendly towards all the many spiritual powers and intelligences which "run" the universe under divine control, then they become friendly towards us, and hail us as a brother or sister. The most exquisite joy comes to our soul when we realise that this is the case, and that we are in a state of love and friendly relationship with every atom, intelligence, entity and being in the whole universe. No wonder our Lord said that we must first be reconciled to our brother before bringing our gift to the altar, and that if we do not forgive those who trespass against us neither can our Heavenly Father forgive us our trespasses against him! It is impossible for us to become attuned to life, and to enter into a state of unity with all the unseen forces of life, if we are not loving and friendly towards all creation. But, as soon as we love sufficiently, we are bidden to enter.

Chapter Eighteen

One Law, One Principle

Some readers may think that life would be all right if it consisted of gazing at flowers, or wandering in the woods, making friends with furry little animals, or joining at daybreak with the birds' dawn chorus, or, as night is falling, their evensong; but, unfortunately they can enjoy none of these things, for they live amidst the roar and clang of trams and buses, and what they want to do is to find the friendliness of life amid these things, and also amongst landlords, mortgages, and noisy or quarrelsome neighbours.

No matter what our circumstances may be, the same law and principle obtain.

Sometimes, it is true, the forces of evil appear to obtain the upper hand. But prayer can bring about a complete divine adjustment. There are angelic powers and beings, who are friendly towards us, who respond to our prayers to the Lord and to High Heaven for help and deliverance.

Thank you for purchasing this book. If you have enjoyed reading it, please consider leaving a review. It takes just a moment, and helps small publishers like us boost the visibility of our books, so that other readers can find our titles. Thank you so much for reviewing this book. We deeply appreciate your time and effort to do this.

You can scan this QR code by holding your phone's camera to the code. A prompt will appear, which will take you directly to the 'leave a review' page.

To review in the UK please scan the QR code or follow this link: https://bit.ly/4jdvzD9

To review in the US, please scan the QR code below or follow the link: https://bit.ly/3WfMnjo

Also by Henry Thomas Hamblin

 The Stillness of the Infinite

 The Message of a Flower

 The Secrets of Your Divine Powers

 The Spiritual Path to True Success

Please visit www.thehamblinvision.org.uk to purchase the following titles:

The Way of the Practical Mystic

The Little Book of Right Thinking

The Power of Thought

My Search for Truth

The Story of my Life

Within You is the Power

Life Without Strain

Divine Adjustment

The Open Door

Life of the Spirit

ALSO BY HENRY THOMAS HAMBLIN

His Wisdom Guiding

The Hamblin Book of Daily Readings

God Our Centre and Source

God's Sustaining Grace

www.ingramcontent.com/pod-product-compliance
Lightning Source LLC
Chambersburg PA
CBHW060619080526
44585CB00013B/894